E-thoughts from The Human Imprint

A collection of thoughts and musings written and posted between June and November 2007

Louise Manning, PhD

©Louise Manning 2007   www.thehumanimprint.typepad.com

ISBN 978 0 95568 320 6

Published by LJM Associates Ltd, The Hill, Castle, Frome, Ledbury, Herefordshire, HR8 1HL UK

Note: This publication is designed to provide accurate and authoritative information in regard to the subject matter covered. It is sold with the understanding that the publisher is not engaged in rendering legal, accounting or other professional services through this publication. If you require legal or other expert assistance, you should seek the services of a competent professional.

Contents

Introduction 5
June 16, 2007 – Communication 6
June 17, 2007 – Educating the Consumer 7
June 18, 2007 – Communication: What is it? 8
June 23, 2007 – Mediation Leadership 9
June, 24 2007 – Business Mentoring 10
June 25, 2007 – Assertiveness 11
June 26, 2007 – Being Effective 13
June 27, 2007 – Change 14
June 29, 2007 – I know it but am I implementing it? 15
June, 30 2007 – Negotiating Skills 16
July 01, 2007 – Talking the Talk 18
July 02, 2007 - Conflict Resolution 19
July 03, 2007 – Do you volunteer? 20
July 04, 2007 – Standing on the shoulders of giants 21
July 06, 2007 – What does my jacket say about me? 22
July 07, 2007 – You just don't get it do you! 23
July 08, 2007 – How often do you retreat? 25
July 09, 2007 – The art of persuasion 26
July, 11 2007 – Latin quotations 27
July 12, 2007 – Are you a good advocate? 28
July, 13 2007 – Chinese Proverbs 29
July 15, 2007 – He who fails to plan, plans to fail 30
July 19, 2007 – Just tell me how much it costs! 31

July 23, 2007 – Is your business on the back foot?..32
July, 26 2007 – Asserting yourself in a team 33
July 27, 2007 – Putting yourself in a good light..35
July 28, 2007 – If you are in a hole stop digging!..36
August 02, 2007 – Why do you have such an attitude problem? 37
August 06, 2007 – Do you have leadership qualities? 39
August 07, 2007 – Are you good at giving constructive feedback? 40
August 08, 2007 – Are you a good facilitator? 42
August 09, 2007 – What is business ethics? 43
August 10, 2007 – Are you good at delegating? 44
August 11, 2007 – Will you just stop bickering! 45
August 13, 2007 - Does the work environment you provide affect employee performance? 46
August 15, 2007 - What is quality?..48
August 18, 2007 - Effective leadership 49
August 19, 2007 - Walk a mile in my shoes..51
August 24, 2007 – Presentation Skills..52
August 27, 2007 – Finding Mentors 53
August 27, 2007 - Organisations with vision 54
September 03, 2007 - Have you made the best of today? 55
September 04, 2007 - Goals, objectives and performance standards..................56
September 05, 2007 - Badges for Achievement 57
September 10, 2007 – Reducing Stress..58
September 16, 2007 - Seize the day 59
September 20, 2007 – Keeping busy 60
September 22, 2007 - International Day of Peace 61
September 27, 2007 - The number seven 62
September 29, 2007 - Individual centred training 63
September 30, 2007 - Does your Organisation have a Corporate Social Responsibility Strategy?..64
October 01, 2007 - CSR Stakeholders..66

October 02, 2007 - Effective training 68
October 03, 2007 - Greek quotes 69
October 04, 2007 - Eight facts about number eight 70
October 09, 2007 - Starting the journey 70
October 10, 2007 - From a town called Searchlight 71
October 12, 2007 - Story Tellers 72
October 15, 2007 - Pioneer spirit 72
October 20, 2007 - Agricultural issues 73
October 30, 2007 - A post on patience 74
October 31, 2007 - Volunteering your talents 75
November 01, 2007 - Living out of a suitcase 76
November 05, 2007 - Facilitating change 76
November 09, 2007 - Received wisdom 77
November 09, 2007 - You're listening to me, but why don't you hear? 78
November 09, 2007 - First impressions 80
November 10, 2007 - Two visionary men 81
November 10, 2007 - Remembering the fallen 82
November 11, 2007 - Collaborative decision making 83
November 13, 2007 - Musing on musings 84

Introduction

This book is a collection of some of the observations and thoughts that were posted to my weblog "The Human Imprint" (located on the web at www.thehumanimprint.typepad.com) between June and November 2007. This form of communication has been a source of inspiration to me over this time and I am sure will continue to be so in the future. They contain musings on the human condition at work and in our daily lives especially how we communicate with each other and the imprint that we leave behind us.

Louise Manning

June 16, 2007 – Communication

Sometimes when we are so concerned about the message we want to communicate we express ourselves in a way that merely turns the audience off. It is very hard when you feel passionate about a subject not to become intense, or appear angry, and then use strong emotive language. It is also often a human reaction by the listener, or group of listeners, as part of the flight and fight mechanism to "shoot the messenger". So I have worked out five tips for myself:

1) Know where your audience are. Do your research and find out what they think and how receptive they are to what you are going to say;

2) Know where you want to take your audience. Can you only take the audience on part of the journey in the time you have? If so, don't try and give the whole message in one go.

3) Be prepared and plan how you intend to facilitate their journey. What are you going to say, what props are you going to use, how are you going to use your time effectively?

4) Think about what questions you could be asked and plan the answers that you might give. Think of the most technical questions and make sure you can access the data either at the presentation or be able to respond quickly afterwards.

5) Don't take things personally, it's the ideas that you are talking about that people may not like, not you.

I'll let you know if they work!

June 17, 2007 – Educating the Consumer

One of the phrases that I often hear in agricultural circles is that "we need to educate the consumer to buy our product"! If we tell them that they must buy our product then they will. I have a real problem with this term "educate" because, whose responsibility is it to educate the consumer and why do we, whoever "we" are, think they need educating? Education is about the imparting of knowledge, but in order to do that the person doing the educating must obviously be knowledgeable! So who are the experts and will the general public trust these, so called experts, whoever they may be either retailers, food manufacturers, farmers and growers, food technologists, nutritionists, celebrity chefs, doctors, academics, politicians, or government employees .... There is a paternalistic assumption in this scenario that others know far more than the consumer does about what is good for them and why they should buy it. Is this true?

As producers, in order to understand our consumer we need to understand what impacts on their individual autonomy and the food choices they make. Social restrictions include: personal circumstances including disposable income, hours of work, shift patterns, literacy skills; availability of options for food e.g. garden produced, convenience store, out-of town retailer, high street; knowledge of health and nutritional information and pressure from other members of the family with regard to food purchase. If farmers do not recognise that all these factors impact on buying choices, they will fail to connect with their customer.

Another definition of education is the imparting of culture from one generation to the next and I think this is actually what some agriculturalists mean. The food we eat and the way that food is produced is imbedded in our culture. We were one of the first countries to experience the industrial revolution in the 1850s so in the UK our urban population has been disassociated from the countryside for over a century. Unless we recognise as producers and consumers the value that our food culture has for us as individuals and as a population we will not be prepared to pay for it if the principles or standards raise costs above global commodity value. Socrates said about education, "I cannot teach anybody anything, I can only make them think." So let's get the nation thinking!

June 18, 2007 – Communication: What is it?

Communication is about the passing of messages from one person to others. In a previous post I thought about how I could improve my communication, but I wanted to take this thought a little further. Communication involves people, passing information between themselves and feeding back on the information and hopefully at the end of the communication taking a resultant mutually agreed action.

In order to communicate effectively we need to consider the language we use and our language can be both verbal, and non-verbal. Often the non-verbal communication has the strongest influence on our ability to communicate with others. This was brought home to me very firmly by my own children. I have always had a home office, but on the days when I was dressed up in a suit about to go off to work - often wearing my coat over the top from 7 a.m. onwards so I would keep clean, my children would get very frustrated, they sensed I was unavailable to them. It was only when they could talk that they began to say to me the minute I came into the house "Put your cuddly clothes on!" i.e. become available to us. When I worked at home, I obviously wore my home clothes - well I didn't have a web-cam! - and they associated the different types of clothes I wore with different activities, although I was essentially the same person.

This taught me a huge lesson, we all take comfort from what is familiar and that includes our appearance, what we wear, our mannerisms and the often deep-rooted opinions that we have, but does this interfere with how others perceive us and also the message that we are trying to convey?

June 23, 2007 – Mediation Leadership

I have had a busy few days and they have left me thinking about leadership and more specifically effective leadership qualities. What makes a great business or community leader?

- Is it someone who leads by the dominance of their personality and because they single-mindedly believe their ideas are the only ones that will work?

- Is it someone who delegates to individuals those tasks they think that those individuals can manage whilst retaining other decisions that only they will make?

- Is it someone who leads through mediation?

Mediation is about leading through reaching mutual agreement that the final decision is the right one for everyone around the table. It is not about leading by compromise, appeasement or dumbing down, far from it! Mediation leadership is about valuing everyone's ideas and reaching consensus after discussion that the final conclusion or action plan is valid and owned by all.

Mediation leadership is about dialogue and communication, qualities that can be lacking in some organisations but underpin others.

Mediation is about identifying areas of current or potential conflict in a management team, or the wider business environment and determining strategies to manage the issues effectively.

Mediation leadership requires personal skills such as flexible thinking, an ability to communicate, empathy, patience, optimism and an ability to listen, but ultimately make a firm decision based on the ideas that they have heard as well as their own beliefs. It also requires leaders to be able to articulate why certain ideas were not taken forward at the close. A leader who says that they haven't got time to listen to those around them is a leader who may end up without any followers!

June, 24 2007 – Business Mentoring

Who are the mentors for the agricultural industry? Where can young or not so young people in the industry find independent and appropriate advice and support?

Mentoring is a management tool that many organizations utilise to support and develop their employees and can be either an informal or an informal process. A mentor is someone, who may be older, but who has more experience, and helps and guides another person's personal and career development. This guidance and support may be proved either internally or externally to the business. At the outset of the mentoring process it is important to define and develop the learning objectives and to then measure progress against those objectives. Finding the appropriate mentor is very important and both parties should be able to quickly develop a positive rapport. Mentors must be prepared to share their experiences of success and of failure and most importantly what they learned as individuals from the experience.

So, where are the mentors in the agricultural industry?

In England, the Fresh Start initiative aims to develop a network of mentors who will be able to offer valuable experience and assistance to those developing new farming businesses. This is a college based scheme for young people, but what about existing businesses and existing employees especially as there is so much change within the agricultural and food supply industry?

June 25, 2007 – Assertiveness

Sometimes it is hard to communicate your feelings without becoming angry or even a little aggressive especially when you feel that others are disregarding your point of view and not taking account of your feelings or opinion. It is important to understand and control how you react to situations of conflict. Sometimes individuals who want to avoid conflict at all costs will become passive and quickly back down from the position they hold or else will not discuss certain subjects with colleagues or line managers. Other members of the team may find it difficult to communicate their ideas and therefore react very negatively when certain subjects arise and use destructive, even aggressive and humiliating tactics to ensure that their needs and requirements are always met over and above those working with them. Issues such as these ultimately affect the management team and the effectiveness of the organisation!

Assertiveness is the ability of either an individual, or a management team, to confidently express themselves and communicate directly in a controlled way their requirements, whilst having empathy with the requirements of others. Body language, such as posture, eye contact, gestures, facial expression and voice speed and tone, also have a large part to play in highlighting to others passive, assertive or indeed aggressive behaviour.

If a quality manager feels that they need to stop a production line because of a quality problem how do they communicate this to the production manager?

- ❖ STOP the line NOW!
- ❖ YOU are ALWAYS messing up and now YOU'VE done it again!
- ❖ I feel WE have a problem; can WE discuss it and agree the actions WE need to take to resolve the issue?

Assertiveness is about establishing your integrity and why you have a right to express your own values, opinions and implement the requirements of your job. It is also about being able to ask for information or assistance, take appropriate time to reach conclusions, or even change your mind without feeling that such a request undermines your position in the team. Team assertiveness is about recognising that as humans we all capable of make mistakes or missing targets and that these issues can be more easily rectified in a positive rather than a negative working atmosphere. Assertiveness is about understanding how a situation will affect others and working out how you can address their concerns and questions in order to ensure they understand why you are making the statement, or decision especially when they do not have any role in the decision making process.

Assertiveness is about demonstrating the positive personal face of management and the organisation internally to other colleagues and externally to your customers.

June 26, 2007 – Being Effective

Ernest Hemingway said "Never confuse movement with action!" In our organisations we are often surrounded by seemingly very busy people, but are they actually being effective?

How do we measure effectiveness and performance of organisations, departments, teams or individuals? Maybe by the length of their working day, or the volume of emails, reports they produce, but are these good measures of effectiveness?

Every individual, team or organisation should develop business performance indicators that are appropriate to respective roles and responsibilities, but what should we measure? Here are some ideas:

- **D**evelop financial measures include return on capital, equity, or investment or operating efficiency;
- **R**eward results not activities;
- **A**ssess behavioural change for positive or negative trends;
- **M**onitor customer and employee satisfaction with performance;
- **A**nalyse how tasks and activities can be done better and improve outdated practices.

After all being effective is essentially being able to produce the intended result!

June 27, 2007 – Change

Mahatma Gandhi said that "You must be the change you wish to see in the world." I remember saying to a friend once that "We must be the people we want our children to be", pretty much the same sentiment. But how do we lead by example in order to implement change? It is not always easy especially if you, as the leader at a particular moment in time don't know exactly where you are going and what others reactions will be when they meet hurdles they believe they cannot overcome. Managing change is about having a structured approach so that you can manage the transition from where you are to where you intend to be. Effective change management requires the engagement and assistance of the people involved and can be defined as follows:

Clarity - making sure all employees are aware that change is going to occur

History - communication of why the change is needed and what will happen if nothing is done

Awareness - of what needs to be done i.e. mapping the journey

Network - implementing a management and resource base to support the journey

Goals - identifying the destination using clear goals and objectives

Empathy - understanding the impact of the journey on others

CHANGE!

June 29, 2007 – I know it but am I implementing it?

Sometimes when I am facilitating group development activities someone in the group will say "I know all that, so tell me something new!" My reaction to this kind of comment, especially in order to develop debate is "If you KNOW it then why aren't you DOING it?" It is often difficult to translate knowledge into effective action.

Using myself as an example I knew as an adult I should learn to swim, especially to ensure my children's safety in a swimming pool. However knowing I should learn to swim and then actually booking some swimming lessons was definitely not the same thing. In the end I took the plunge physically and metaphorically speaking and had some lessons and once I had got over the FEAR of the water I actually enjoyed it and reached my target of being able to swim a mile!

What held me back for twenty years? As with all barriers to taking action they are multifaceted, what would I look like in a swimming costume after having three children, looking foolish perhaps with the other people in the group, actually most of the people in the swimming group were grandparents learning to swim so they could swim with their grandchildren, and they were trying to learn sixty years too late, so I needn't have worried. My biggest problem though was as I have already said FEAR and that made me recognise what a strong, and irrational, human emotion it is.

When you say to yourself well if I know this why am I not implementing it, ask what do I actually fear? Is it fear of failure; is it fear of success because that will change the status quo? Is it peer group pressure, because you are not sure how the team will react? In a management situation it is so important for us to recognise this real human concern because so often it can make us inert and unable to grow and develop as individuals, teams or organisations and take effective action.

June, 30 2007 – Negotiating Skills

One of the key life skills to acquire is the art of negotiation. I am much better at interacting with people on all levels of my life since I learnt the basic art of negotiation. I am not saying that I am a fully fledged negotiator but I am getting there slowly, and who taught me this life skill? My children!!

It is a steep learning curve when faced with an individual with limited vocal communication skills, due to their own degree of personal development, who can only identify their needs through body language and either how the volume or the pitch of their shouting. Actually that sounds quite familiar in some business situations I have been in!

When individuals lack the life skill of being able to calmly vocalise their feelings, or point of view they will quickly switch to secondary means of communication. Some individuals miss out the first step altogether and go straight to expressing themselves emotionally.

These issues impact on management's effectiveness, and we must consider them when having to facilitate or negotiate with, or within, operational teams. When negotiating with(in) teams and with individuals we have to understand the visual signs that tell us how people feel towards either each other or the information that is being presented, including changes in the:

- ❖ Pitch, speed or volume of their voice,

- ❖ Eye contact - who are people looking at, who looks down when certain people speak, this will help you to identify the level of agreement and disagreement within the meeting/team

- ❖ Nodding and smiling – who smiles and nods in compliance with some views and sits stony faced when others are talking.

- ❖ Hand gestures – banging a fist on the table is an obvious sign but are all the people expressing open hand gestures or is there the overall impression that everyone in the meeting either has their fists clenched or their arms firmly folded. Do hand gestures change when different people speak?

If you are the manager, team leader, or facilitator it is important to constantly consider these cues during a meeting. An effective manager will identify where they are in terms of the five point plan, see below. Effective negotiation management is about continually rating where you are on the scale – if the meeting starts to go to a 3 rating you need to take action to reduce down to a 2 or below. If the meeting gets to a 4 you need to take immediate action before the meeting gets out of control, even if it is to announce a five minute coffee break to reduce the tension. Do you have this life skill; if not what steps are you going to take to acquire it?

The five point plan is basically how would you rate the meeting at this moment in time (1 = In control meeting, going totally as planned, 2 = in control, some side debate, but on track, 3 = in control, but increased side debate and some individuals starting to exhibit emotional behaviour, 4 = starting to lose control, people starting to talk over each other and meetings objectives are in danger of not being achieved. 5 = everyone's lost the plot and the meeting objectives are effectively abandoned.

July 01, 2007 – Talking the Talk

When you communicate with your colleagues at work, do you consider whether you talk at them, to them or with them? The question may sound pedantic, but if you want to create accord within an organisation or team it is important to consider how YOU communicate.

When people talk at each other, they each try to control the conversation, wanting only their opinion to be considered and totally dismiss the others point of view. People who talk at you rarely listen to your reply, it just isn't important to them. One extreme example is the way a prosecution and defence lawyer will talk to each other, each resolute that only their opinion is of value.

When you talk to people, it implies that you have the superior opinion and in some business communication that is indeed the case. You could have to make the final decision and then communicate that decision to the team or work force. The decision itself is often non- negotiable and the method of communication has to emphasise this. When talking to people there should always be an element of listening, but it should be emphasised at the beginning that the discussion element is only to clarify points or overcome confusion not to change the decision.

A conversation is about talking with and listening to people in equal measure. It recognises that during the conversation everyone's opinion is equally valid and everyone should be given equal time. The discussion should be open, with each person talking in turn, and keeping to the point. It is very important that the person managing the conversation ensures that the ground rules are defined, understood and complied with by all. A conversation and effective drawing together of the conclusions will increase ownership of the ultimate decision, because people believe they have been heard and can understand the valid business reasons if an alternative decision has been reached.

Well how do you communicate, can you improve? Are you talking the talk?

July 02, 2007 - Conflict Resolution

When you communicate with your colleagues at work do you consider whether you talk at them, to them or with them? The question may sound pedantic, but if you want to create accord within an organisation or team it is important to consider how YOU communicate.

When people talk at each other, they each try to control the conversation, wanting only their opinion to be considered and totally dismiss the others point of view. People who talk at you rarely listen to your reply, it just isn't important to them. One extreme example is the way a prosecution and defence lawyer will talk to each other, each resolute that only their opinion is of value.

When you talk to people, it implies that you have the superior opinion and in some business communication that is indeed the case. You could have to make the final decision and then communicate that decision to the team or work force. The decision itself is often non- negotiable and the method of communication has to emphasise this.

When talking to people there should always be an element of listening, but it should be emphasised at the beginning that the discussion element is only to clarify points or overcome confusion not to change the decision.

A conversation is about talking with and listening to people in equal measure. It recognises that during the conversation everyone's opinion is equally valid and everyone should be given equal time. The discussion should be open, with each person talking in turn, and keeping to the point. It is very important that the person managing the conversation ensures that the ground rules are defined, understood and complied with by all. A conversation and effective drawing together of the conclusions will increase ownership of the ultimate decision, because people believe they have been heard and can understand the valid business reasons if an alternative decision has been reached.

Well how do you communicate, can you improve? Are you talking the talk?

July 03, 2007 – Do you volunteer?

Have you developed your personal skills through undertaking voluntary work? Could you develop your career through a portfolio of voluntary activities?

I undertake a range of work for charity or community groups primarily because I want to make a difference and I like giving something back to my community that in turn supports me.

When I reflect on the tasks I have undertaken I have also gained a lot of experience which then has helped or enhanced my working life. This includes planning projects, chairing groups and committees, team building, public speaking, understanding the range of motivations of individuals and groups, overcoming areas of conflict, negotiation skills, designing goods and services and marketing those goods and services, publicity management etc. etc

Many individuals have turned a hobby into a career, by starting their own business and selling goods and services that were originally a part time pursuit.

Undertaking voluntary work can also open your horizons and help you to find purpose, feel involved and actively contribute, explore your own strengths and develop new skills and make you proud of what you can achieve. Those new skills may enhance your current job role or may provide you with a springboard to move on to a new area of your career.

What are the barriers to you using volunteer work as a way of meeting personal needs and developing your skills and talents?

Many would say lack of time, age or level of education and all of these may be good reasons for not volunteering, but for others these are just excuses for inactivity. Think again about volunteer work because it might just supply you with the experience you need to fill a gap in your resume!

July 04, 2007 – Standing on the shoulders of giants

Is humility a trait that should be developed in business? What skills does it afford the effective manager?

In 1676, Sir Isaac Newton wrote "If I have seen further it is by standing on the shoulders of giants" in a letter to Robert Hooke a fellow scientist and mathematician. I think that this is a really amazing statement in which he is attributing his successes not just to himself and his intellect, but to those around him who have provided help and support. It shows a great degree of humility.

Humility is about respecting others, for if you don't respect others how can you expect them to respect you? It is at the other end of the spectrum from character traits such as aggressiveness, arrogance, self-absorption.

Many organisations covertly develop and promote these latter skills believing that they will benefit the business, but do they are we really "seeing" as far as we could be? If we surround ourselves with people who primarily do not represent a threat to us, we do not develop and grow ourselves, because our ideas are not challenged and honed.

Choosing work colleagues who do not provide complementary and additional talents to our own reduces the future development and current effectiveness of the organisation, and ultimately reduces our ability to delegate tasks and activities. Standing on the shoulders of pygmies doesn't have quite the same ring to it!

Humility is about being confident in your strengths and talents, but recognising the limitations of those abilities. Humility reduces conflict and minimises disputes, and builds teams rather than cliques. Ultimately, it defines the wise leader rather than the self-focused empire builder.

July 06, 2007 – What does my jacket say about me?

Do you always act based on first impressions? In other words, do you judge a book by its cover?

In previous posts, I have recounted how I wear different clothes in different situations, but what do my clothes say about me? My wardrobe is divided into clothes I wear to work, clothes I wear at home and clothes I have to wear if I expect my children to walk down the street within five paces of me! All items projecting very different images and expressing either others, or my perception of who I am.

I have realised that subconsciously I will wear different colours or clothes depending on the impression I wish to create and how I want to effectively manage a meeting. Some colours will signify leadership and dominance, others will express co-operation and team work. I often ask myself, what about the clothes other people wear? What are they trying to signal to me, the team or the organisation? It is said that you make your first impression within three seconds. Have a look in the mirror what do those three seconds say about you? Do they say what you want them to say?

However, it is true that you **can't always judge a book by its cover** and it is important to remember that before you make a judgement you should consider the evidence that is supporting your decision and whether it is valid, as the old saying states marry in haste, repent at leisure! The true value of an individual is not always obvious from first impressions because sometimes people guard their talents and skills. The art of management is knowing who is who!

July 07, 2007 – You just don't get it do you!

How do you get your point across in a discussion or meeting? If people don't appear to be getting the message do you just shout louder?

We have probably all been in the situation where we are lost and ask for directions. The person giving you directions knows where they are, where you wish to go and how to get there, but can they communicate that effectively? All too often someone has given me an elaborate description of how to get the mile or so I need to travel and I have politely thanked them and then had to ask someone else because I didn't comprehend a word they said. The next person might have drawn a little map with arrows on a scrap of paper and I have been able to reach my destination in minutes. Why was that? Was it because I wasn't listening intently enough to the first person, because I hadn't asked for a map the first time or just because the first set of instructions weren't in the right language?

Language is the system of communicating with others using sounds, symbols or words. We use language to express our ideas, thoughts, a vision or new concept and to provide a sense of meaning. Nelson Mandela said, "If you talk to a man in a language he understands, that goes to his head. If you talk to him in his language that goes to his heart." As communicators, we firstly have to make sure we are talking a language people recognise, then if we are talking a language someone understands and finally if we are talking in their "own" language. If we do not create "ownership" of the language then we will not carry the audience.

If I am talking to a group of young people, would I use the same language as if I was talking to a group of adults in their forties, no I wouldn't! The current debate on climate change is a perfect example of the effect of the ownership of language. If politicians and scientists talk to us in "their" language are we fully engaged by the discussion of policy, taxation and global targets? Probably not – if we see photographs of mountains, rivers, glaciers before and now, if we see graphs and graphics we may begin to understand some of the issues depending on the strength of the argument and the abilities of the communicator. However what does it take for us to have ownership of the language and for it to become our issue? It's when the parents waiting with us outside the school, mates in the pub, family, friends or neighbours discuss that they are changing their car, going on holiday by train, starting to grow their own fruit and vegetables, bought a compost bin that we truly begin to engage.

I remember the upbeat song "Free Nelson Mandela" by the special A.K.A in 1984, it was a song that instantly engaged young people in a way other forms of communication did not and it made the calls for his release suddenly "their" issue and demonstrates the immense power of talking to someone in their language.

July 08, 2007 – How often do you retreat?

How often do you retreat? We all need to recharge our personal batteries, but do we do it enough?

Retreating in its spiritual or religious sense is about taking time away from everyday life and reflecting and seeking to find answers to the issues or problems that we face. Retreat, or quiet reflection, as a thought process helps us with our personal lives, but can also help us in business. How noisy is your office space, are you constantly being interrupted when you are trying to think through ideas? Are you encouraged to leave enough time for quiet reflection in your working day? Meetings can be very good to air views and opinions and reach a consensus, but a trap that many organisations fall into is to end up having a meeting to discuss what you they are going to discuss at the next meeting and so on and so on and never making any decisions.

Peter Drucker said that we should, "Follow effective action with quiet reflection. From the quiet reflection will come even more effective action." Is everyone expected to think on their feet in your organisation or is there space in the day for people to undertake quiet reflection? When project timetables are developed is the need for reflection incorporated into the design process i.e. having time to "sleep on it"? Have colleagues been trained in the art of quiet reflection and is this valued as a management process?

How many times has your organisation decided in haste and repented at leisure? If the answer is "Too many times!" then maybe you need to consider incorporating this management process more effectively into your corporate style!

July 09, 2007 – The art of persuasion

Are you good at persuading others to see your point of view? What methods do you use to influence people?

Persuasion is the process of appealing to individuals and guiding them in accepting an idea, thought or action. It is a means of problem solving that uses rational processes and is based on appealing to an individual's powers of reason, their emotions, and should not be based on force or coercion, especially if you wish them to take ownership of the final decision. The Ancient Greeks suggested that there were three elements to persuasion, namely ethos, pathos and logos.

Ethos is about the person who is communicating (or persuading) and whether they can create empathy with their audience i.e. does the audience buy into their ethical credentials and believe they are trustworthy, and credible, if the audience does not believe in the character of the presenter they will not listen to them or allow themselves to be persuaded. **Pathos** is the factor that motivates the audience and means that once the audience trusts you they will then emotionally connect with the message. It is important to consider the factors that will either motivate or indeed alienate your audience and ensure that you can engage the audience with the appropriate motivational factors. **Logos** is the element of reason, which you use to reinforce the emotional engagement and provides the justification to your audience for why they should agree with you.

So when you are putting forward an argument or point of view, do you normally consider these three elements? If not, next time you are preparing a presentation think about:

Having

Ethos

Logos and

Pathos

It really will **help** you to focus it on the needs of your audience and improve your skills of persuasion.

July, 11 2007 – Latin quotations

Sometimes I use Latin quotations in management presentations for a bit of fun and to focus attention on key themes in the presentation, here are some of my favourites:

- *Quo vadis?* Where are you going?
- *Cui bono?* To whose profit?
- *Acta non verba.* Action not words.
- *Audio, video, disco.* I hear, I see, I learn.
- *Consummatum est.* It is achieved.
- *Carpe diem.* Seize the day.
- *Die dulci freure.* Have a nice day.
- *In nuce.* In a nutshell.
- *Mutatis mutandis.* The necessary changes having been made.
- *Pecunia in arbotis non crescit.* Money does not grow on trees.

If you like them, then use the phrases in your presentations too.

July 12, 2007 – Are you a good advocate?

As a team leader you often have to be an advocate and speak on behalf of another person or group of people, so how good are you at communicating the needs and expectations of others?

An advocate is someone who supports another person either by speaking on their behalf, or by helping them to communicate their own thoughts, feelings or ideas. Advocates need to have inter-personnel skills, be effective communicators and negotiators; be able to understand and implement the balance required between listening to people and talking; and between advising a course of action and allowing individuals to discover their own solutions to the issues that they need to address. Advocates must also be sensitive, diplomatic, and use discretion with individuals and their team. Successful advocacy therefore contains elements of both mentoring and coaching. Indeed, as team leaders this is one of our key responsibilities if we want our teams to remain positive and function well.

Whilst we can often be a good advocate for another person, we also need to be able to practice self-advocacy. Self-advocacy is our ability to effectively communicate, argue and assert our needs, rights and best interests. In order to be effective self-advocates we need to have self-knowledge and honestly identify our:

- Strengths and weaknesses;
- Rights and responsibilities; and
- Needs and aspirations;

As individuals we therefore need to make informed decisions and also take full responsibility for those decisions. Do you have the skills to be a good advocate?

July, 13 2007 – Chinese Proverbs

Following the post on Latin sayings here are some Chinese proverbs which will stimulate conversation in a meeting or presentation:

- Teachers open the door. You enter by yourself.
- Seeing once is better than hearing a hundred times.
- A journey of a thousand miles begins with a single step.
- He who asks is a fool for five minutes, but he who does not ask remains a fool forever.
- Experience is a comb which nature gives us when we are bald.
- Be not afraid of growing slowly; be afraid only of standing still. It is not the knowing that is difficult, but the doing.
- Men trip not on mountains they trip on molehills.
- An ambitious horse will never return to its old stable.
- A spectator sees more than a player in the heat of a game.

I think all of these may be titles of future posts!

July 15, 2007 – He who fails to plan, plans to fail

How good are you at planning? Are you a thorough planner or the kind of person who thinks on their feet, maybe you are someone that falls somewhere in between?

Planning is the process of defining aims and objectives, developing strategies and setting goals and then determining the distinct tasks and timescale that it will take to accomplish the aims, objectives and goals. How do you determine strategic plans for your organisation? What mechanisms do you use to communicate those plans effectively throughout the business?

Many organisations develop a network of "to do lists" and "action plans", but simply keep regurgitating the same issues and keep moving them from one list to another never closing any out. Do your action plans initiate effective action or just sit on a desktop and gather dust until the next review?

Take a look at your business plan and ask these questions, is it a strategic plan that outlines the vision and direction of the organisation? Have you planned where your business will be next week, next month, at the end of the year or five years time? Do you develop the framework strategy into an operational plan that defines realistically how the strategy is going to be implemented, breaking the activities down into distinct responsibilities and focused tasks with measurable performance indicators?

Effective implementation of strategy requires an organisation to have the right balance of individual plans in all departments and at all levels of the organisation and these plans must then interrelate and cross-reference too. It is important to determine who in the organisation is going to co-ordinate the activities and ensure that the relevant personnel have adequate resources, training and support to understand, take ownership of and implement the strategy and operational plans. There must also be a defined feedback mechanism so that weaknesses, problems and failure to meet targets and milestones are identified and prompt action taken to resolve the issues. Appropriate contingency plans should also be in place to address organisational risks that could impact on the successful implementation of the strategy.

Lots of questions, but do you have all the answers?

July 19, 2007 – Just tell me how much it costs!

Increasingly we live in a world where we know the price of an item or service, but do we know its true value?

There is an old English saying that we can "know the price of everything, but the value of nothing" and in our all-consuming, "I want it now", society this saying still has great relevance. When I walk around the supermarket I am bombarded with the offers "half-price", "buy one get one free" otherwise known as "BOGOF", "30% extra" and so on, but what does this actually mean to me, the consumer?

Take the case of fresh strawberries, they seem to have been "half-price" all season, in fact I am sure I have yet to see a punnet without a half-price flash. Do we as consumers actually remember what we paid for our strawberries last year? I don't, but perhaps I could rummage around and find an old till receipt that would tell me. Does the "half-price" flash make us buy more strawberries even though they are always badged as such? Well it certainly attracts our attention as shoppers and make us feel that this could be the good "deal" we've been looking out for! Our eyes instinctively always go to the part of the receipt that tells us what we have saved today on the special offers. If it is a BIG number we feel duly gratified, even if it means we have actually spent more money than we intended or that a week later we throw much of the food away because it has then gone out of date.

If a product is always discounted, how long is it before the reduced price becomes the "actual" price? When a product is always sold at a reduced rate will this eventually devalue it as a commodity for the consumer?

Do we consider the actual production costs of our purchases? We all start to become uncomfortable at the point of purchase if our attention is drawn to issues such as animal welfare, use of global resources, worker welfare or fairness of trade with suppliers, even more so if we are actually required to make an ethical decision. The problem with ethics is that whilst it is a good idea in the abstract sense, when we are sitting watching television reports, planning corporate social responsibility strategy or having a drink with friends, in the actual sense when it starts to hurt our pockets or require us to implement change then suddenly it isn't as clear-cut. So, whilst we seem to care about the price of our purchases, do we care about their true value?

July 23, 2007 – Is your business on the back foot?

A proactive business is one where the management team work well to identify specific circumstances or issues that could affect the business in a positive or a negative way and determine how they can be effectively managed. Indeed a proactive organisation is one that plans for the future and gains commercial advantage from such activities whether this is leading the market rather than merely following other competitors in their field, one that drives the current market and anticipates and leads change. A proactive organisation is also one that anticipates the skills and abilities it requires in its workforce and takes steps to ensure that those skills will be available when that business needs them.

However sometimes the steam can go out of a business, personnel change, strategies drift and the business starts to lose its edge, and instead of being proactive it becomes passive and starts to only react to situations.

Reactive businesses react to events when they are actually occurring and tend to try to manage only that particular issue without having the time or resource, and sometimes the actual inclination to do anything different. As a consequence reactive business often evolve an organisational hierarchy with complicated sub-structures and overly bureaucratic systems because they are always problem solving at, or after, the event and rather than doing the leading themselves in the marketplace are being led by the decisions and behaviour of their competitors.

So what kind of business is your business? Is it proactive or reactive or somewhere in the middle? Are some departments in your business proactive, whilst others are reactive and is this currently creating conflict within the organisation? Firstly, you need to recognise that this is an issue for you, secondly determine how deep-rooted the problem is and then thirdly how you are going to redress such concerns before they affect the bottom line and ultimately before it is too late for your organisation!

July, 26 2007 – Asserting yourself in a team

How often do you find that others in the team take over and you can't seem to get your point of view across? We have all been involved with team activities where one person likes to take control. If they are not the team leader this can very quickly affect the dynamics of the team and negativity can set in. What can you do to assert yourself and your views in this situation? Here are some ideas:

- Prompt the team leader to reconfirm the scope of the teams activities especially if individuals are straying from the proposed plan;

- Ask the team leader to clarify the aims and objectives of the team especially at a meeting if they are losing control. Remember to be calm and assertive rather than aggressive;

- Give everyone else a chance to state their views and where possible lose some of their momentum;

- As they talk write down the key words they say in two columns for those words you agree with and those you don't;

- Choose the right time to speak, this can vary but a good time is when most people have had their say and before the team leader starts to conclude the activity;

- When you speak use the key words that you have written down when putting your point of view. Make eye contact with each individual in turn when you agree with what they have said and use "their" key word. This will make them more likely to concur with your comments;

- Try to conclude as you speak so that you put forward an argument on why you agree with some points and not with others. This will validate your point of view and may sway those who when they first put their point of view across did not agree with you; and

- Refer to the aims and objectives of the team or meeting and how what you are putting forward meets those aims and objectives;

If you can achieve all of these steps and still appear calm, confident and non-confrontational this will help you to carry the discussion. It will be your words and logic that will be ringing in the ears of the team members as they discuss and agree the actions to take. Avoid at all costs being drawn into open combat or territory that you are not familiar with and being drawn into negativity or being belittled by others.

Remember, you allow yourself to be belittled or ignored, if you don't value your own opinion, how can you expect anyone else to?

July 27, 2007 – Putting yourself in a good light

Self-branding is a frequently used word, but how good are you at promoting yourself? What does your personal profile or curriculum vitae (CV) say about you?

Increasingly, we have to "sell" ourselves to potential employers, clients, customers and work colleagues. We can quickly run into trouble if we over-promote ourselves and then cannot deliver and at the opposite end of the scale we can continually sell ourselves short. So what is the best way to describe what we can offer?

We often use a personal profile or CV to describe our abilities and strengths. In the past curriculum vitae contained very precise information, personal details, schools attended, qualifications including grades and the examining board, previous job experience and referees who would vouch for our good character and work ethic. However, the tone and content seems to be changing over time. I read a number of CV and the same layout even the same font seems to appear again and again, it is though the applicants have been formulated to fit the template rather than the CV designed to promote the person. There are often huge unexplained gaps, off travelling perhaps, or a job that the applicant doesn't really want to talk about?

Within the personal profile you often find the series of bullet points on the benefits and character traits the applicant will bring to an organisation. The same words seem to circulate, everyone is committed, ambitious, energetic, strategist, always delivering and meeting targets, hardworking, conscientious. Certain character traits such as calm, focused, empathic, able negotiator, team builder, mentor, coach, enabler rarely appear. Why is this? Is this because the people developing their personal profiles do not believe these skills are worthy, or because they don't believe their potential employers or clients consider them important? Will the personal blog eventually supersede the CV because with this medium the client or employers could gain a greater insight into the thoughts of the person?

So have another look at your personal profile, what does your self-branding actually say about you, what skills are you promoting and are they those that your "market" needs?

July 28, 2007 – If you are in a hole stop digging!

Sometimes you dig your own hole and promptly fall in it, on other occasions someone digs the hole for you and you merely oblige. So what do you do if you are in this situation?

Back to the hole! You need to recognise that the how you got in the hole is history! Whilst hindsight is a good thing, especially if you use the experience not to make the same mistake twice, once you are in the hole how you got there is largely immaterial, it's how you manage to get out that's important! So what do you need to do?

(a) Recognise that you are in a hole;

(b) Stop digging! Don't make the hole any bigger than you have already;

(c) Work out the dimensions of the hole and how big a problem you have;

(d) Determine if you are on your own in the hole or if you have taken others with you;

(e) If you are with other people agree a plan of action that utilises the best of everyone's skills; and

(f) If you are on your own logically plan each step of how you get out and limit potential damage.

All too often in business we are in denial, either pretending or not wanting to recognise that we have made a mistake or trying to cover it up. This eventually makes the initial problem worse. Individuals and organisations then compound the problem by develop strategy upon strategy to address the "non-issue". We can only learn from our mistakes if we recognise that we are fallible as individuals and as organisations and have an open culture that supports admitting mistakes and learning from them.

August 02, 2007 – Why do you have such an attitude problem?

Do you find that other people always have a problem communicating with you? Do you find yourself wondering what's wrong with them and why can't they just get their act together? Conflict occurs at many levels within an organisation, team or between two individuals. How does conflict initially arise?

Normally, conflict occurs because there is a divergence in views or opinions on what has happened, **the facts**, where you are going, **the aims, goals and aspirations**, how you get there, **what methods and measures you take** to complete a course of action and **ethics** i.e. the values or boundaries that exist for your or the group's behaviour i.e. what is acceptable or unacceptable practice.

In many situations conflict occurs as a result of subconscious behaviour and often the individuals concerned are unaware of how they actually reached the point where they are at loggerheads with others. Often we assume that it must be the other person who has the problem and that we don't do anything ourselves to cause the conflict. However, before you accuse another person of having the attitude problem ask yourself if any of these apply to you – do you:

Always believe that you are right and only your opinion matters;

Tough it out and refuse to give way on any issue;

Threaten others in order to get your own way;

Instantly react in a situation, never count to ten first before responding;

Talk in a sarcastic or cynical way to others;

Undermine others so that their position is weakened;

Don't hold anything back; say anything that comes into your head;

Explode in anger when you think that others let you down.

OR

Praise the positive, before discussing the negative in any situation;

Resist the need to use anger when you feel you are losing control;

Orchestrate how you argue a point so that it appears to be a win-win result for everyone;

Base your approach to others on how you wish to be treated yourself – with respect;

Listen to others and then explain clearly and calmly why you disagree with them;

Empathise with others and understand why their approach is different to yours and determine how you are going to reach consensus;

Manage communication effectively.

So the next time you are heading for conflict ask yourself who is it that has the problem?

August 06, 2007 – Do you have leadership qualities?

The leadership qualities required to make you a good leader can vary in different scenarios, work teams or organisations. Do you have the skills required to be a good leader?

Leadership is the setting and implementation of a strategy or vision within an organisation or group and the ability to drive where required behavioural change to see that strategy through to its conclusion. Leadership qualities include:

L - letting others express their views in a positive environment and then being able to make a decision based on the needs of the strategy and their views;

E - expressing yourself clearly, calmly and giving clear directions;

A - assisting others in the team or organisation to identify actual or potential problems and implement appropriate solutions;

D - delegating responsibilities to others whilst also ensuring that they have the skills, abilities, knowledge and understanding to complete the tasks;

E - empathising and showing appreciation of the contribution of others in delivering the required outcomes;

R - respecting those in the organisation as you yourself would like to be respected;

S - setting goals and objectives and communicating those with clarity to others;

H - harnessing creativity in individuals and teams;

I - involving the whole team in the implementation of strategy;

P - promoting integrity and corporate values and ethics;

So, do you have the skills required to be a leader?

August 07, 2007 – Are you good at giving constructive feedback?

Are you good at giving constructive feedback? If not, what stops you from assisting those who work for you to improve their performance or formally recognising their successes?

As managers we are often required to give feedback on other people's thoughts, ideas and performance. If we have not received positive or constructive feedback ourselves in our working lives or personal lives we can often find it difficult to give appropriate feedback ourselves. Giving constructive feedback will not undermine the person giving the feedback in fact it usually enhances their position as a manager or mentor, whilst shouting, bemoaning, dismissing or disrespecting individuals will negatively affect the way a manager is perceived. So, how do you give constructive feedback?

- ❖ Prepare for the discussion and plan what you are going to communicate. Group the issues into positive, neutral and negative categories so that when you give feedback it well constructed, has clarity and good flow. Determine if you are going to address all the issues in one meeting or discuss the main issues in the first meeting and then address the others in a follow up meeting;

- ❖ Give positive feedback as soon as you can after the event – don't leave feedback too long otherwise it will lose its benefit to the individual and the organisation. If the whole management team/workforce has contributed to success then give feedback to the whole team or workforce. If you always feedback only to the senior management team then you may find that the feedback does not actually cascade down to other colleagues. Consider giving global constructive feedback in team briefings, company newsletters or on wage slips;

- ❖ If you have to give negative feedback, don't do it when you are angry or cross as it can quickly escalate into areas where you did not intend the discussion to go. Ideally give negative feedback on a one-to-one basis and never in front of fellow workers or in a public forum as this may well belittle the individual concerned, create negativity in the management team and encourage others to believe that such behaviour is acceptable within the organisation;

- When giving feedback make sure that all the comments that you make can be substantiated by fact, otherwise points that you raise could be challenged by those who do not accept the information or decision that you have made;

- Always start with something positive when you give feedback and address the key issues first, so be direct and don't go around the houses to get to the main point of the discussion. The person will probably already think they know why you have asked to see them;

- Reinforce the key issues and ask the individual how they think they should be addressed, negotiate mutually agreeable solutions where possible;

- Ask the individual receiving feedback if they need you to clarify any points and if they understand what you require them to do; and

- Finally, end on a positive note!

August 08, 2007 – Are you a good facilitator?

You may be able to chair meetings or manage team projects, but do you have the skills and ability to be a good facilitator?

If you are the manager of a team or chairing a meeting you may well lead the meeting or project to move in the direction that you want them to go in and seek to influence decisions so that they comply with your personal aims and objectives, this is not facilitating. Training too differs from facilitation in that the trainer takes the lead role and in many ways can dictate what the learning objectives and learning outcomes are and drives the communication process in order to achieve that process. So we have defined what facilitation is NOT, then what is it?

On one level a facilitator is a person who makes things happen e.g. is an organiser or provider of administration services. However, a business facilitator is a person who is an **enabler**, i.e. someone who provides others with the ability, means or opportunity to find their own solutions to problems or issues. They can also be a catalyst to develop strategy or implement organisational change. Facilitation is an acquired skill and the ability to facilitate effectively improves more and more with experience.

A facilitator is a good organiser with regard to meetings, developing agendas, keeping records of discussions and interactions effective time management and driving effective communication especially of any specific actions that are required with responsibilities and timescales. They must be able to define and at times bring the group or meeting back to the aims and objectives of the interaction and the planned outputs. They need to enable others to communicate with respect and also be able to understand human interactions and how conflict can be resolved. They must be able to assist all individuals to make an active contribution to discussions and use a range of questions in order to stimulate discussion and assist participants to reach appropriate conclusions. Facilitators must be able to intervene effectively and if agreement cannot be reached, assist individuals or teams to understand the reasons why there are differences of opinion and the options available to seek to reach consensus. In short facilitators must be good communicators, flexible, able to think on their feet, sensitive and unbiased; well do you fit the bill?

August 09, 2007 – What is business ethics?

We hear the word ethics in business more and more but what does it actually mean? The word "ethics" comes from the Greek word "*ethos*" meaning conduct, customs or character. Ethics addresses the implementation of concepts such as responsibility, right and wrong and the application of moral ideals to practical human activities.

Ethical analysis will address the constraints of moral standards and legal requirements and the consequences of actions. The output of such analysis is the determining of principles and protocols, the development of individual and group responsibilities and the verification of the outcome of the implementation of such a framework. Individual countries, cultures and business organisations will determine distinct codes of ethical behaviour. Individual organisations therefore need to determine their ethical strategy and the scope of such strategy may include the following:

- ❖ Criminal behaviour and the need to operate within the legal framework. The strategy may include awareness training for individuals and teams so that employees understand the legal constraints on the business and the responsibilities this places on individuals;

- ❖ Human values and personal behaviour. Ethical policy needs to define at a strategic and human resources level how people are expected to behave both internally within the business and also in their interactions with suppliers, customers and competitors and the development of business relationships;

- ❖ Behaviour in business. Ethical policy should address how all corporate activities are undertaken, monitored and verified to ensure that they comply with legal guidelines and ethical standards. Ethical strategy should also include a review of potential ethical business risks and how these can be mitigated.

So what is your organisation's ethical strategy and does it stand up to scrutiny?

August 10, 2007 – Are you good at delegating?

I often hear managers say that they work such long hours because they don't have anyone to delegate to. If you are in this position, do you know why? The benefits of being able to delegate are obvious. Effective delegation can save management time, motivate staff and aid personal development amongst colleagues. Weak delegation will lead to the opposite and cause conflict, demotivate individuals, especially if they feel they are being overloaded and ultimately business goals and objectives may not be met.

Delegation is a key management skill and it is important to recognise that whilst the manager or supervisor retains overall responsibility for the aims and objectives it is the individual who has the responsibility for achieving them. There are varying degrees of delegation and the manager must give some thought to the extent of autonomy an individual will be able to cope with. It is important not to give too much freedom, especially if the individual you wish to delegate to has neither the skills, ability, and knowledge nor the level of training required to manage the task effectively. It is also important to confirm with the individual what degree of autonomy they feel they adequately handle before delegating any tasks.

So why can't you free up your time by delegating some tasks to others? Is it because you are worried that they can complete the task more quickly or more efficiently than you and thus put you in a bad light? Do they lack specific skills that you alone possess or that you just don't trust them?

Trusting colleagues requires a manager to become vulnerable to the actions of another colleague whilst having confidence that the colleague will undertake the task even if the manager's ability to monitor or control the individual is at times constrained. You need to ask yourself why you don't trust your colleague and how you can develop consistency in your working relationship. Theodore Roosevelt summed this up by saying that "The best executive is the one who has sense enough to pick good men to do what he wants done, and self-restraint enough to keep from meddling with them while they do it."

August 11, 2007 – Will you just stop bickering!

Many of the "great" disaster movies start with a group of people bickering and falling out until a monumental event occurs normally a flood, hurricane, volcanic eruption, and they all pull together to reach their common goal!

I notice with my own children that whilst there is an unwritten code that allows them to bicker, carp and argue among themselves if an "outsider" is negative in any way towards one of them then there is suddenly a consolidated front and it becomes the three of them against the world!

These two examples demonstrate that bickering occurs in most human groups and many managers allow an ongoing banter within their team that can have both positive and negative overtones. The benefits of team interaction include cohesion of the management team and the development of working relationships and mutual interests, but when does bickering actually become bullying?

Organisational culture often supports mild ribbing, joke making but should never accept a situation where such behaviour crosses the boundary to either bullying or victimisation. Observers of such incidents can also be seriously affected by what they see, hear or witness, especially if they are powerless themselves to intervene. Workplace bullying can exist at many levels and can result in reduced job satisfaction, self-esteem and a poorer opinion of the organisation itself with those who are affected and ultimately a lowering of operational performance. Health problems can occur for observers and the individuals concerned including headaches, anxiety, and depression.

As a manager, you must always give a clear, unequivocal indication of what is acceptable behaviour within your team. Managers must remain aware that individuals do not always react in the same way to jokes and ribbing and that there are workplace boundaries on such activities.

It is important to keep an eye on colleagues and open a dialogue with them if the health problems outlined persist during the working day. Bullying is never acceptable and managers must lead by example with this regard to ensure that they promote, and themselves comply with, high standards of behaviour within the organisation.

August 13, 2007 - Does the work environment you provide affect employee performance?

Are you sure that the environment that you provide for your staff to work in doesn't affect their performance?

The environment that people are required to work in can have a significant impact on their ability to undertake the tasks that they have been asked to do. This can affect productivity and employee health and well-being.

The key factors fall into two categories, those that are driven by procedures, protocols and management requirements and the factors that arise from premises, office or factory design.

Management driven factors include the development of:

- Organisation plans such as the allocation of responsibilities at all levels of the organisation, definition of job descriptions and the degree of access to the management and administrative support needed to complete their tasks;
- Working patterns, shift-working, break times, absence or holiday cover; and
- Health and safety policies, including the provision of training, development of safe working practices and the adequate supply of protective clothing and equipment.

The work environment can also have an impact on an individual's ability to work safely, competently and in compliance with operational performance targets. It is important to address the following:

- Work space availability. Have you determined whether there is adequate space available for the tasks the individual is required to undertake? Are desks/computer terminals being shared and is this affecting productivity or causing stress? If the individual is working in a manufacturing area and they need to complete documentation or carry out inspection is there a work station available in their work environment close to where they work?

- ❖ Light intensity. The requirements for light intensity and type of light should be determined as insufficient light will impact on visual inspection activities.

- ❖ Weather/temperature. Is the area where the individual is required to work too hot or too cold, open to the weather/elements? If there is a requirement to work outside or in adverse temperatures does the company provide adequate controls, clothing or equipment?

- ❖ Ventilation/humidity. Does the work environment contain poor quality air that could cause fatigue or a reduction in performance?

- ❖ Noise/vibration. Can vibration affect an individual's performance or safety? Is it a requirement to wear ear protection? Could this adversely affect performance?

- ❖ Odour/dust or other emissions. How is this assessed and if required controlled to ensure personnel safety?

- ❖ Premises hygiene/welfare facilities. Is the area that the individual is expected to work in hygienic, clean and tidy? Does the level of clutter affect performance? Is the area so filthy, unhygienic or infested with pests that it causes stress to those individuals working there? Are staff facilities, toilets, washrooms, canteens, coffee making facilities appropriate and maintained in a hygienic state?

How often do you as a senior manager take a site walk? What do you look for? Do you know what effect current employee dissatisfaction has on organisational productivity and profitability? Remember it is your responsibility to ensure the health, safety and welfare of those who work for you!

August 15, 2007 - What is quality?

There are lots of different ways to describe quality in fact people have written books or PhD thesis on the subject. Every person will probably have a slightly different opinion - "the best you can buy", "consistent - the same every time you buy it", "meets my specification", "value for money" and so on. Basically "quality" is firstly understanding what the customer wants in terms of products and service and then consistently giving them what they want. If you give your customers what they want at a price that makes you a profit, then you have a viable business!

Sounds easy, but then it becomes a bit more complicated, because as an organisation you need to work out who your customers are. There may be a number of external "customers" in the supply chain for example, manufacturer, distribution company, retailer, wholesaler, and consumer. Legislative bodies or assessment bodies are also external customers and their requirements need to be met. As well as external customers an organisation has a series of internal customers each department in turn from goods inwards to production and despatch as well as other services, administration, sales, marketing, human resources having a discrete set of requirements that it needs to have met. Before a documented quality management system (QMS) is developed an organisation must not only determine who their customers are, but also the aims and objectives of their organisation i.e. what they are setting out to control with their QMS. Documented systems that are developed to cover issues such as quality assurance, human resources, health and safety and/or environmental issues are often called integrated management systems or IMS. So where do you begin:

- ❖ Know who your customers are:
- ❖ Understand what they want from you;
- ❖ Determine how you are going to meet their requirements;
- ❖ Identify the management protocols that need to be in place to control the system;
- ❖ Deliver what they want, when they want it and for a price that delivers a profit!

August 18, 2007 - Effective leadership

Peter Drucker once said that "Management is doing things right; leadership is doing the right things". In our working life it is important to decide whether we are capable of being effective managers or great leaders. We all want to be leaders but do we have the required skills?

Clearly successful managers need to have well-developed organisational skills and provide clear direction, develop goals and objectives and ensure their team meet deadlines. They must be able to delegate tasks and responsibilities and create a productive working environment where acceptable standards of behaviour have been clearly defined and are rigorously enforced.

Effective managers also need to have good communication skills and be able to present their ideas in both formal and informal situations. They should be able to discuss their ideas, listen to others, whilst offering, and sometimes accepting themselves, constructive feedback.

Managers should also be able to facilitate the sharing of ideas, and the resolution of any disagreements or situations of conflict. So what makes a great leader? A leader is a person who:

- Inspires by example;
- Maintains credibility and engenders the trust and confidence of those who work for them;
- Demonstrates a respect for all those who work alongside them and the contribution the tasks they undertake make at all levels of the organisation;
- Promotes the values and mission of the organisation with colleagues, suppliers and customers;
- Develops ownership among colleagues for the work they undertake and the goals that need to be achieved;
- Motivates others in a positive way, often without the individuals themselves realising; and

- ❖ Ultimately makes everyone feel that they have a clear, distinct and achievable vision for the future.

So are you a manager or a leader?

August 19, 2007 - Walk a mile in my shoes

I was listening to an Elvis tribute programme on the radio last week and they played a song of his that I had not heard before entitled "Walk a mile in my shoes" written by Joe South. The lyrics of the song have stayed with me during the week and has made me consider how good we are at seeing things from other people's perspective and whether we consciously try to understand other people's points of view and why they behave in a certain way or make certain decisions.

It is very easy to make a judgement about someone when we first meet them or first hear someone talk about them or once we get to know them if they suddenly change in some way.

We use a range of cues to assist us often visual, e.g. their appearance, degree of self-confidence, mannerisms, tone of voice, or body language and our intuition is affected by our past experiences with others who may have behaved in a similar manner. Once we have made such an evaluation we often take a lot of persuading to change our minds.

Have you ever sprung to criticise someone before you have taken the time to understand their point of view? How often have you gossiped or commented about a work colleague's erratic behaviour or said something inappropriate to them that you later regret when you find out that they have had a recent bereavement in the family or are going through another kind of personal problem?

It is so important for all of us to take the time to mentally walk in "their" shoes, understand what pressures they are under and why these concerns could be affecting their work performance. As managers we need to work with them to find ways to deal with or resolve these issues when they arise. Remember with your management team YOGOWYPI – you only get out what you put in!

August 24, 2007 – Presentation Skills

So you were asked to give a presentation and on the spur of the moment agreed. Is time running out and are you beginning to wonder if you have made a monumental mistake?

Where do you start with the presentation? Well, first find out the title and the key points you are expected to address. It is very important to find out who else is talking and what they are going to talk about. You want to make sure that you do not cover exactly the same ground as someone else; otherwise the audience will just get bored. Determine how long you are going to be asked to talk for as this will help you to work out if the time you have means you can only give an overview or whether you are required to give an in-depth presentation of your topic. If you only have time for an overview then identify what you **must** say, what it would be **good** to say and the points that you will address only if you have time.

Try to think about how many slides you will have on a PowerPoint style presentation. If you are not comfortable with the technology design 3 or 4 slides that are general and will cover several themes so you don't need to change them that often. If you are using slides or overheads limit the technical data as you don't have the slides to be too busy. Remember graphs or data tables are a waste of time if either people can't see them at the back of the room or they haven't time to read them during a presentation. Don't put too many bullet points on each slide; consider using diagrams or photographs instead of words if they convey your message, because they are much more effective.

Practice what you are going to say and check the presentation before the day, especially if someone else has prepared it. There is nothing worse than standing up in front of an audience with a presentation full of typing errors or slides in the wrong order.

Most important of all believe in what you are going to say, because lack of conviction comes over to the audience immediately in a presentation. People will forgive beginners nerves but they will struggle with a presentation that lacks personal belief or one where the presenter just reads from the slides parrot fashion – well they could have read it as a handout themselves! Show that you care about the topic and remember practice makes perfect.

August 27, 2007 – Finding Mentors

Do we find our mentors or do our mentors find us? What do you look for in someone who can help you improve your skills and talents?

Speaking personally, the people in my life who have helped me develop my personal and professional skills seem to have largely found me rather than the other way around.

A senior executive once said to me "Well you don't sow your seed on unfertile soil do you, because it is simply wasted!" I think he meant that if someone does not have the capacity to develop and learn either as a result of their intellect, skills and abilities or the mental ability to accept that they have always have more to learn and that they may sometimes have made a mistake which they have to accept, learn from and move on, then they are not worth mentoring.

Everyone's resources are limited in terms of time and energy and we should not waste them! Many of my mentors have been outside of my working environment, people who have shown me how to approach life in a different way, or with a new perspective, how to prioritise my daily schedule and the demands people place on me and I am still learning!

A mentor is often described as a wise or trusted counsellor, this means that they must have life skills and have actually experienced and dealt with some of the issues that we now need to address, not just have read it in a book or been told it in a training seminar. Whilst many people can give advice some good some bad, much fewer can impart wisdom. So how do we recognise wise words?

Well I think that first we have to have trust in the person that they value us and the impact that their words will have on us and our future. We also have to trust that they do not have any other vested interest in influencing our behaviour, and that is not always easy to determine at the beginning of a mentoring relationship.

Mahatma Gandhi said that "a teacher, who establishes rapport with the taught, becomes one with them, learns more from them than he teaches them." This is true with a lot of the mentoring that I undertake working with others and we have to be open to new experiences and new ways of doing things. So choose your mentors well and if they choose you then be open to their teaching!

August 27, 2007 - Organisations with vision

How do you recognise organisations with corporate vision? Is the organisation's corporate social responsibility policy produced as a result of commercial one-upmanship or as a result of deep ethical foundations within the organisation?

Politicians are in a cycle of ever increasing their environmental credentials over and above their opponents, but does this encourage voters to actually change the environmental impact of their personal lifestyle?

Nearly every day corporations and business organisations are declaring their worthiness with regard to social responsibility, food safety, environment impact, personnel health, safety and welfare, fair trade and ethical supply chains in a variety of reports and policy statements. Third party standards have also been developed that address many of these issues and organisations continue to increase the portfolio of certificates that they display in their reception areas and on their websites. What impact does all this have on the purchasing decisions of the consumers of their products and services?

Mahatma Gandhi said that "An eye for an eye leaves the whole world blind..." so does this suggest that the constant declaration of improved and enhanced corporate ethical credentials leaves consumers and customers non-plussed? Does the psychology of we will worry about the environment, employee health and safety, etc. when you do, leave us all inactive and weaken organisations by increasing their business risk?

Consumers and customers must be able to trust the integrity of organisations and their brands and if this is based on claims and statements of intent then these criteria must be measurable otherwise performance cannot be verified and ultimately that trust may be lost.

There are a growing number of organisations where ethical standards are embedded in goals and organisational aspirations, organisational and departmental structure, job descriptions, and brand marketing is firmly based on these standards where actual performance can be measured and verified. Organisations that produce policies and associated reports without such foundations run the risk of undermining the very equity of their brands.

September 03, 2007 - Have you made the best of today?

Today is September 3rd, 2007 - can you say that you have you used your time effectively today? How would you feel if you had lost a day or even ten? In 1752, in England and the American States, people went to bed on the 2nd September and woke up the next day on the 13th of September, because England adopted the Gregorian calendar. There was no September 3rd that year!

We all work according to our calendars, task lists and schedules - what if they were shifted by ten days - would it matter, would it actually affect the organisations we work for? How would you prioritise what needed to be completed and what could stay at the end of your list for another day, week or month? Do you spend so much time making lists, amending lists or checking emails, or alerts or mobile phone bleeps and rings, or having meetings about meetings that you don't actually get any work completed?

I spent a day analysing how many times I clicked the button to "check up" on some electronic message or other and realised that if I double the time period between checks I could probably save an hour a day. Some people have a real adrenalin rush when the little envelope appears in the corner of their multiple electronic screens, but do we need to check or reply to them instantly?

If this is proving a problem for you, how are you going to address it?

September 04, 2007 - Goals, objectives and performance standards

In the eight weeks that I have now been keeping records this site has been visited by people in over 50 countries! This is a statistic that I find totally staggering, especially as I was unsure as to what goals and objectives I should have for The Human Imprint when I started posting. It also demonstrates the power of the internet and blogging particularly as a communication tool. As with any other personal or life tools whilst some people will embrace the positive benefits others may see ways to use it in a negative way. I have had my own problems with spam blogging over the last month or so, and thank you to The Podcast Sisters for discussing the issues in so much depth in their latest audio show, with lots of positive tips on how you can watch out for the "culprits" homing in on your articles or posts.

Statistics .... We all have performance indicators that we develop to measure our performance on a personal basis or in our working lives, but how do we develop them? Are they based on what our family, friends or work colleagues are doing, achieving or planning to do or what they think we should be doing? Do we measure ourselves against targets that can never be achieved? Think about the work place because this can be the same with organisational goals, objectives and the associated policies and strategies. Who in the organisation is responsible for making sure that there are sufficient resources to achieve those standards, assuming they are the right standards for individuals, teams and the total organisation in the first place? We spend our lives setting guidelines, monitoring them for success and then revisiting the original targets and many times starting again. Does the effort that we expend actually drive the business forward or could we utilise that resource in other areas to greater benefit?

Are we auditing the auditors, who are auditing the auditors, who are auditing the auditors, who are .....

If so, what is this actually delivering to the organisation?

September 05, 2007 - Badges for Achievement

Well, I have spent the last two days at various intervals sewing! I can see when I survey my handiwork why my needlework teacher (that ages me as it is now design and technology!) said I wasn't a suitable candidate for Needlework O Level! However, I can't say either that not having this qualification has vastly affected my life choices, but getting back to the point I have been sewing on name tags in the children's school uniform and also their achievement badges. There is something about a school uniform that tries to create conformity and yet the children themselves create their uniqueness through their expression of their personalities. A school uniform also gives a sense of belonging to a community something all humans need to feel in order to thrive.

As I was sewing the myriad of achievement badges onto blazers, sweatshirts and other items, I thought about the feeling it gives us when we are rewarded for success whether that is a simple thank you or a badge, certificate or even financial bonus. When I see my children smiling as they remember what it took personally to achieve each badge I question whether we do enough in our organisations to recognise people and the contribution they make.

Do you say thank you to the person who has stayed late to help you finish an assignment/project, or made coffee for the meeting? Do you call someone and thank them for their part in a recent success? When we view ourselves and each other for what is positive then it benefits everyone and the organisation too!

September 10, 2007 – Reducing Stress

Well, I can't believe that it is five days since I last wrote a post for this blog. We all get times when we have literally too much to do, not enough hours in the day, and we have to prioritise.

Sadly, the blog was put on a back-burner for a few days. The reason that we get stressed is that our priority list doesn't agree with our partners, our family, our community, work colleagues etc etc. It is hardly surprising that all these "To Do" lists are different! It is then that we start to feel the tension rising and we need to have our de-stress strategy ready. How do you de-stress - we are all different, but here's what I do. In a stressful situation I will

- Mentally count to ten, slowly and precisely,
- Make sure that I am breathing properly and deeply and say nothing if it is going to make the situation worse,
- Analyse if the people around me are in control of themselves, if not try to help them gain control, or
- Suggest a period of time to withdraw from the meeting/discussion to regain composure.

So in essence I gain control and help others to regain theirs.

At the end of the day we should all have a calming ritual. The Japanese Tea Ceremony is a ritual that is designed to calm and relax and in developing our own process we will help ourselves to leave those stresses, thoughts, worries behind. With children you are encouraged to have a routine - bath, drink, story, bed time in a room that has been designed not to over stimulate, when do we start to break that rule for ourselves as adults?

What can you do on your journey home to relax, certain music, audio book, novel, newspaper. If we take our stress home with us then it quickly becomes contagious!

September 16, 2007 - Seize the day

Well, being English I never thought I would be cheering on the Georgian Rugby Union Team, but last night I was on the edge of my seat wondering if they would deliver a giant-killing defeat to Ireland in the Rugby Union World Cup.

Why was I shouting for Georgia, well because of a friend, whose name was Tim Attridge. Tim, who sadly is no longer with us having died several years ago spent time in Georgia and Tajikistan probably ten or fifteen years ago now. As well as working on a number of projects, he helped to set up some Rugby Union teams. He felt the sporting ethos especially that of Rugby Union that catered for all shapes and sizes in one team could transcend differences and difficulties and help to create mutual support and teamwork among a group of individuals.

He once wrote to me about the young men that were learning the game who were turning up to train, many of them unable to afford the bus fare who were walking there and back as well as training for the games. He also said that they expressed great determination, resilience and spirit in their tackling and forward play, never giving up and committing themselves totally to everything they did. Well, last night they proved him right in every way - Tim's life's tenet was "Carpe diem" - seize the day and they certainly demonstrated that - a lesson to us all.

September 20, 2007 – Keeping busy

Thomas Edison is reported to have said that "Being busy does not always mean real work. The object of all work is production or accomplishment and to either of these ends there must be forethought, system, planning, intelligence, and honest purpose, as well as perspiration. Seeming to do is not doing."

Again this week time seems of a premium and it means that I haven't been giving myself my own time to ponder on a subject that comes to mind and then write a post on it. I have relied on my rule of time management this week, and the week before actually and ..., one I honed when I was running a business with three children under five:

- Is everybody fed, watered, clothed and content in the house or work environment?
- Have I done all the things I **have** to do today?
- Have I determined all the things I **have** to do tomorrow?
- Have I got a list of the things I **need** to do if I find time?
- Make sure I don't worry about everything else.
- If I need to, calmly explain why my list of priorities may be different to someone else's and then negotiate how we resolve it.
- Enjoy what I do, and do what I enjoy!

Well, I think the last point is probably the title of another blog post!

September 22, 2007 - International Day of Peace

Yesterday, 21st September, was the International Day of Peace. I wouldn't have known about it at all if my children hadn't brought a letter home advising on the ways that they could mark the day.

What did you do? Well on reflection perhaps I didn't do as much as I should have done, but none of my friends, colleagues mentioned the word "peace" at all and the day seemed to slip by. I thought about how we create peace at home, at work or school and I have written before about having places for quiet reflection in the work-place where we can go to think through problems, strategies and how we address work issues before communicating our conclusions to work colleagues. Sometimes in the workplace when we see someone sitting quietly, thinking, we assume that they are not working - they are daydreaming, but this is often not the case.

Environments can over stimulate in terms of noise, colour, smell, activity and this will affect our ability to work and problem solve. I love working in public libraries. Sometimes I take my laptop to a library to work, because of the peace and quiet - no telephone, no emails and I can think! I also give myself some time to look at books in a section that I wouldn't necessarily naturally migrate to - it is amazing how refreshed you can be when you come out, rather like after doing some yoga, and meditation.

Do you provide a peaceful place in your work environment? Do you provide a tranquil place for your children to do their homework? Do you turn all the radios, televisions, computer games off for a certain period of time each day so everyone in the house can experience peace and even talk to each other about their day, the issues they have to address? Do you spare a thought for those around the world who are unable to experience peace in their homes and living environment?

Martin Luther King encapsulated this thought when saying "Peace is not merely a distant goal that we seek, but a means by which we arrive at that goal".

September 27, 2007 - The number seven

What is so special about the number seven? If you go into the business and lifestyle section of a book shop seven must be the number most widely used in the titles - "7 steps to ...." "Seven ways to ..." Why does it seem that seven is appearing so frequently even in blog posts- well here are seven reasons why the number seven is interesting:

- Seven is a lucky number!
- Seven is the fourth prime number;
- There are reportedly seven virtues and seven deadly sins;
- Common ladybirds have seven spots;
- There are seven stellar objects visible with the naked eye Sun, Moon, Mars, Mercury, Venus, Jupiter and Saturn and there are seven stars in the Ursa Major constellation;
- Seven hills of Rome and seven wonders of the ancient world;
- There are lots of films with seven in the title - Seven, The Magnificent Seven, The Seven Year Itch, Seven Brides for Seven Brothers, and of course Snow White and the Seven Dwarfs.

Well whilst it is a bit of fun, I sometimes use this exercise at the start of a training course or team building forum as it is a way of breaking the ice and getting people to start to communicate with each other. The answers will also help you to assess whether they are individuals who think and work in numbers, words or pictures. This is an important factor for a facilitator or mentor to determine so that they can deliver effective support. Give it a go...

September 29, 2007 - Individual centred training

Leading on from the previous post, I have over the last year evolved my methods of training and mentoring. I have changed the way I support individuals and develop materials since I read the book by Temple Grandin, on "Thinking in Pictures". I was lucky enough to go to a conference on Autism in May in the UK and hear Temple Grandin speak. Although I am very interested in her work on animal welfare and understanding how animals think, it is her thoughts on how humans learn and communicate that have had the most effect on me. She was talking at the conference specifically about suiting individual jobs and organisational roles to a person's abilities, strengths and weaknesses.

We each have our own methods of thought processing, and we may use either visual or verbal thought processes. Often we will have associational thoughts and wonder how we began thinking about ice-cream and ended up thinking about the neighbour's car. We then realise it is because everything we thought about was the colour red and the colour was the factor our brain used to make sense of the range of information. This is an example of visual thinking. Visual thinkers are great at computer programming, photography and design, or solving engineering problems.

I am a verbal, language based thinker. I love using words to express what I think and would naturally produce a paragraph of text to say what could easily be demonstrated by a picture or photograph. I just feel more comfortable using that medium. I am not the least bit practical. I have no spatial awareness so if I had to assemble a piece of furniture I would have to follow the instructions word by word and if they were wrong I would struggle to overcome them to finish assembling the piece correctly. I must take this into account if I am required to undertake a practical project and make sure that I have visual thinkers with me in the team, to create balance and be able to be effective in completing the project. So when I design training courses I also have to recognise that it must meet the needs of both verbal and visual thinkers. I also have to remember that what might be easy for me to understand as a language based thinker is quite the opposite for a visual thinker. It has made me change my training aids and the way I work with people quite radically. So next time you plan a presentation or a training module, think about the thinkers, otherwise many people may just not understand the message you are trying to convey.

September 30, 2007 - Does your Organisation have a Corporate Social Responsibility Strategy?

What is your organisation's direct and indirect impact on its stakeholders? How can you measure it effectively? An organisation has a direct impact on its stakeholders namely suppliers, customers, work colleagues, and consumers of its goods and services. It also has a range of indirect impacts on non-governmental organisations and an indirect, but often significant impact on the local community within which it operates, and on the national or indeed global community. It is therefore important for an organisation to recognise its responsibilities to its suppliers, customers, and staff and address the way it impacts on its social and physical environment.

Organisations need to review their current performance, determine if their current level of performance meets predetermined ethical aims and objectives and if necessary identify how the organisation could improve and communicate this to their stakeholders.

The management team need to define these aims and objectives so that they can drive internal improvements, potentially decrease the cost of production and also build the confidence of customers and potential customers in the organisation. To be a preferred supplier they must inspire trust and confidence by consistently meeting the quality standards of their customers, ensuring reliability in meeting product and service requirements, and seeking to continuously measure and improve performance. They must also be able to demonstrate their understanding of the ways that their activities affect the local community.

A Corporate Social Responsibility (CSR) Strategy can deliver brand value and increase brand equity by acting as a management tool to:

- Manage and where possible reduce costs,
- Manage, mitigate or minimise risk, and
- Identify new organisational opportunities.

Therefore a CSR strategy describes an organisation's vision - its key aims, objectives and measurable indicators of success. It also defines an organisation's governance structure and the management systems that are in place.

Many organisations produce an annual report to inform their stakeholders of their CSR performance and report is increasingly being utilised as a marketing tool as well as an organisational driver. So, how do you define your organisation's key environmental, social and economic priorities? How do you measure business success?

October 01, 2007 - CSR Stakeholders

What are your stakeholders looking for your organisation to address in its corporate social responsibility strategy?

Any corporate social responsibility strategy (CSR) must be fully integrated with the organisation's brand management and commercial strategy. This means that the CSR strategy must support the underlying commercial requirements for the business and deliver to its customers or the ultimate consumer safe goods, products and services that are fit for purpose and deliver optimum quality, optimum price and the expected level of customer service. Internal and external stakeholders are increasingly becoming more concerned about the way an organisation delivers its commercial and marketing.

Ethical objectives that need to be embedded within the CSR element of organisational strategy include:

- **Service related issues** - service design, management of customer care initiatives, quality assurance and sustainable sourcing and supplier approval, ethical trading protocols;

- **Product related issues** – product design, quality assurance, quality control, sustainable sourcing and supplier approval, ethical trading protocols;

- **Operational issues** – management of resources including raw materials, land, energy, water, control of waste produced as a result of activities, including disposal, packaging recycling strategies, management of logistics including transportation of goods and product distribution strategies;

- **Colleague issues** – development of social policy and practice including worker facilities, terms and conditions of employment, personal welfare, health and safety, training and development;

- **Community issues** – management of the organisation impact on the local, national or global community including environmental issues, such as noise, smell, visual impact, use of resources, production and disposal of waste;

- **Brand and organisational risk management** – management of legislative, commercial, operational and brand risks

Does your organisational strategy address all these areas or do you need to revisit your management of CSR?

October 02, 2007 - Effective training

I went to visit a company to discuss their training and development policy and how effective it was and whether there were any improvements that could be made to improve organisational performance.

First I spoke to the management team and the training administrator about the training that they undertook and looked through the systems and protocols for recording the training activities. All looked well and they talked a good talk.

I then spoke to some of the employees about the training that they had recently attended. We got onto the subject of ladder safety training. Using this as an example, we talked through how the course had gone. It was office based and the instructor went through all that you needed to do to make sure that you climbed a ladder safely.

A little tongue-in-cheek I asked if they had actually climbed a ladder at the end of the course to demonstrate competence! To my dismay the individuals remarked that they hadn't had any practical instruction and also had not used the prescribed equipment in the workplace since and as such had not remembered much of the training at all six weeks later. So, how effective was the training?

Well there were lots of certificates in the file, the training matrix was completed with the ticks in the right boxes, but had the trainees actually gained any knowledge and would the training prevent any future accidents?

Confucius is reported to have said that "I hear and I forget. I see and I remember. I do and I understand."

A critical quote to remember for all trainers, mentors or coaches - it is an easy option to deliver training by telling people what they must do. It is not so easy to provide support to people whilst they find out how to do something for themselves when they still have you around to correct their mistakes.

So don't be fooled by all the completed tick boxes and certificates of attendance in the file - go out into the work place and check the training has been effective.

October 03, 2007 - Greek quotes

Following the posts back in July on Latin sayings and Chinese proverbs, here are some Greek quotes that will stimulate conversation in a meeting or presentation:

- Never discourage anyone...who continually makes progress, no matter how slow. **Plato**
- Wise men talk because they have something to say; fools, because they have to say something. **Plato**
- Talk sense to a fool and he calls you foolish. **Euripides**
- One swallow does not make a summer. **Aristotle**
- Haste in every business brings failures. **Herodotus**
- Learn to walk before you run. **Anonymous**
- Do not count your chickens before they are hatched. **Aesop**
- Skilful pilots gain their reputation from storms and tempest. **Epicurus**
- Words empty as the wind are best left unsaid. **Homer**

October 04, 2007 - Eight facts about number eight

After the post on number seven, here are eight facts about number eight in no particular order:

- 8 is a composite number being divisible by 1, 2 and 4. Eight is also two cubed or 2^3, and is the first cubed prime and a number in the Fibonacci sequence;
- A fallen or lying down 8 is the symbol for infinity;
- There are eight known B vitamins;
- All arachnids have eight legs and an octopus has eight tentacles.
- The Eight Immortals are Chinese deities;
- Scorpio is the 8th astrological sign of the Zodiac;
- There are eight furlongs in a mile and eight pints in a gallon;
- "Eight maids a milking" is the gift given on the eight day of Christmas;

October 09, 2007 - Starting the journey

Well, yesterday I came out to the US to start my five week Nuffield Study tour. It was a long day of travelling and waiting around in the airports which got me thinking about new beginnings and journeys - often a time when we feel at our most vulnerable. There were some very stressed people sitting around the terminals. I hope that I learn so much not only about my topic but about many other aspects of life in the US.

October 10, 2007 - From a town called Searchlight

Yesterday I had the opportunity to listen to Senator Harry Reid speak at Brigham Young University. I was struck as I walked into the building by the size of the auditorium which you just wouldn't find in at a UK university. There were several thousand students attending to listen to him. I was struck by him as an individual and also the story of his life and the humble beginnings that he frankly described in Searchlight, Nevada and what he had gone on to achieve so far in his life of public service.

It made me realise that it is always best to gain information or experience first-hand. When others tell us about a fact or issue they naturally filter the things that were important to them, or they think will be important to us - when you experience or communicate directly there is no filtering effect, except our capacity to listen. In the words of the African Proverb, "One must talk little and listen much".

October 12, 2007 - Story Tellers

Today I spent some time in a museum and my attention was captured by the display on storytellers. The display was about the Native American people and how story telling was such a part of the Pueblo culture. The elders would encourage the children to gather around and listen as they, the elders, told them stories. These could have been stories that they themselves had learned when they were children. Story telling was the way they passed from generation to generation the folktales, customs, and their religion.

So who are our storytellers today? Who will pass our heritage from generation to generation? We may not get others to gather around us literally any more, but can we do it virtually? Whilst face to face communication is the best when telling a story, will blogging become a version of Pueblo story telling tradition? We will have to wait and see.

October 15, 2007 - Pioneer spirit

Whilst in Utah, I have heard many stories about brave pioneers. One particularly amazing one I was told by a descendent was about his ancestor who was totally blind and walked across the plains with a hand cart. I can't begin to imagine the strength of character that that requires! I flew across from Chicago in a few hours - it took them months to come across to Utah. An amazing story which will put some of the future challenges I may face truly into perspective.

October 20, 2007 - Agricultural issues

I have spent the last two weeks in Utah, studying water issues and how they relate to development. It has been interesting for me that so many of the issues that we face in the UK are the same here, such as growing urban population, less emphasis on agriculture and the need to produce food and agricultural products, and growth of amenity and tourism activities to support the leisure time of the urban population. Universally, food production seems to be of less and less importance - is this a critical policy mistake? Land prices close to urban areas for land sold for development makes the returns for agricultural production non-viable and many family farms are realising the asset value of their land. In Utah 80% of the water utilised goes into agriculture compared to around 3% in the UK and the demand for water for urban development potentially impinges even more on agricultural production here. There is an old western saying "You can steal my horse, even take my wife, but don't touch my water!" - food for thought I think.

October 30, 2007 - A post on patience

Today, I had a rather enlightening, although not unusual experience. I had to post some of my study materials home, well 18 lb in weight of study materials to be precise! I carried the parcels to the post office for 9 am and the post office was shut. People came in moaning and trying the door, although you could see it was shut. In fact within 30 seconds of some people arriving they were intensely angry that things weren't going their way.

Most stormed off in disgust after demanding information from the other people waiting. My parcels were too heavy to charge too far .. so I resolved that I would stay put and just take my parcels to my meeting if I had too. After 10 minutes the man came out from the office and said that he couldn't open the safe! He was more than a little STRESSED and he said that he would send for reinforcements and hoped the post office would be open in a further ten minutes. Again there was much huffing and puffing and moaning and people having a go at him.

On my study I have been told of women walking four hours every day to get water for their children these people couldn't weight ten minutes!

True to his word he started the day and everyone surged to the door. He told them that he would assist the person who had waited the longest first .. Me! That didn't go down too well nor did our chat about his day hopefully getting better from this point on as he sorted out my parcels.

Courtesy doesn't cost anything. When someone is doing their best and the problem is out of their control, why let off steam at them? It won't change the situation - the post office will still be closed, the train will still be late. I had used my time in the queue to prepare for my meeting and I turned up prepared and calm and the meeting went well. I wonder how those irate people around me approached the rest of their day.

October 31, 2007 - Volunteering your talents

During my time in Utah, I really saw the value of volunteer work, not just to the organisations that depend on the resource, but also for the people who were volunteering their time and their talents at all stages of their lives. I saw the benefit to individuals of giving their time and skills, gratis, not only because they had a sense of having given service by helping others, but also a feeling of self-worth, because they had found inside themselves a personal gift or skill. They had a sense that their skill was valued and in turn they themselves felt valued.

I work with community groups at home and I know how important that feeling can be personally and to the community as a whole. We all need to feel needed. Self-worth is a fundamental part of the human spirit. If we lack self-worth we often feel that we can alter this by "receiving" gifts, buying ourselves clothes, food, gifts, a better house, a more expensive car, but the truth is that we only gain self-worth and self-esteem by giving.

Self-worth is also only attained by self-acceptance and identifying our strengths and our vulnerabilities. Giving of our time, our talents, our experience and wisdom, or even just listening when someone else needs so desperately to talk is truly valuable.

If we don't value ourselves how can we expect others too?

November 01, 2007 - Living out of a suitcase

I have lived out of a suitcase for three weeks now on my Nuffield study tour. I have worn my four sets of clothes in every possible combination. Some hotel rooms I have felt very comfortable and at ease. Other rooms I have felt uncomfortable and I just don't know why that was but just had to make do. Travelling has been a lesson in life for me on what you REALLY need for a journey and what it is nice to take along. I can only pull or lift a case that weighs 40 lb, so that is what I am limited to take. I must have sent three times that home in books and notes that I have collected on my journey as I have gone along.

It has been the same with time management. I haven't had enough hours in the day at times with travelling, planning the next part of the trip, meetings, writing up notes etc. I have had to categorise things into

Critical - next hour

Urgent - today

Pressing - this week

Soon - on the trip

Rather like my suitcase, I have had to define my limits and focus on C-U-P-S. Maybe I should keep this priority list going when I get home!

November 05, 2007 - Facilitating change

American philosopher and designer Buckminster Fuller is reported to have said that: "You never change things by fighting existing reality. To change something, build a new model that makes the existing model obsolete."

I read this quote this afternoon and found it very thought provoking. I have been on my Nuffield Study tour looking at water policy and it had been driving me to a conclusion, if I can't change the existing models, define a new sustainable one that makes all the others obsolete! That is certainly the challenge.

November 09, 2007 - Received wisdom

Today, someone put the 'phone down on me and it was rather a shock! My call was not unsolicited; I had been invited previously to call back. However, I had only just introduced myself and asked if it was a convenient time to speak when there was the distinct click as the receiver was put firmly down.

There is something very cold about a dead 'phone line when you are left holding a piece of equipment that is no longer functioning. It is as if you have been summarily dismissed by the other person. I retraced my words and decided that it was my name that caused the problem. I imagined the receiver coming away from the recipient's ear and descending downwards by the time I said the word "convenient".

The whole episode got me thinking about politeness. Had he been polite? Not really, would it have hurt him to be polite for a couple of minutes? It is a character trait that is often undervalued especially in this world of short and often terse texts and emails.

Many people just cannot find the time to give someone five minutes of their attention. There is nothing worse than being at a conference or party and the other person is talking to you but constantly looking over your shoulder for someone better, or more advantageous, to chat with!

Today was just a one off incident. Mainly, I come into contact with people who are kind and polite and make you feel that although they are very busy and their time may be valuable you are worthy of that time. I think that you in turn are then respectful of them. When someone opens a door for you, or vice versa, when someone says please and thank you it makes a difference. If someone fills the photocopier with paper for you, changes the water bottle on the water machine it makes a difference. Our lives may just touch someone else's for a brief moment, but we can choose whether we are mutually enriched, or not.

November 09, 2007 - You're listening to me, but why don't you hear?

I have spent a lot of time these last few weeks talking about talking. It may sound a strange statement, but we often hit a metaphorical brick wall when we try to communicate a new idea or thought to other people. Why does this happen? Is it because we just don't articulate our thoughts and views well enough? Have we prepared badly and/or not used the right vocabulary for the audience? Is it that people aren't prepared to "hear" what is being communicated to them?

We might listen to a different perspective or point of view to our own, but are we prepared to hear it, to measure the content and then objectively make a decision on the content?

In a meeting or presentation, we can with the right technique encourage people to listen, but do they hear and then understand our point of view or modify their behaviour? We need to be able to engage our audience and develop a dialogue. The dialogue must of course be two-way we also have to listen and "hear" the response and potentially modify our behaviour too if we are at fault.

Many of the issues we face globally are complicated and not always clear-cut such as climate change, food and water security, dietary and health choices.

An expert lecturing and scolding will often entrench behaviour and does "nanny" always really know best? People accept the message when they trust the messenger, so who is the right messenger? Will we trust experts, scientists, politicians, maybe not if they cannot demonstrate that they are one of us, and definitely not if they don't lead by example. If someone flies in a private jet to deliver a message on climate change does that devalue their message to their audience?

These ethereal issues are often not the most pressing that people face. If you are too frightened to walk alone where you live because you fear for your safety then going to the recycling centre isn't high on your list of priorities. If you have to feed a family on a limited income, it will often affect the products that you can busy no matter how much "advice" you receive on healthy eating.

Only when global issues are discussed within the context of daily life and not as a separate agenda will people become engaged. Only when we demonstrate our worth, our understanding, and our empathy will we finally cease to devalue the message we are delivering and then we will be effective.

November 09, 2007 - First impressions

When you sitting on a train or on a 'plane, or eating on your own in a restaurant, you can't help but look at the people around you. I think humans are innately social beings rather than solitary. You can only glance at them for a second otherwise people start to shift in their seats, because they feel that you are starting to invade their personal space.

How often have you imagined what people are like just from that brief observation? If I am bored on a long journey I will often do this. We may use certain clues to help us in this quest, what they are wearing for example, and I have blogged on this before. We might make assumptions based on what they are eating, or maybe reading an English classic novel, a certain high-brow newspaper or magazine or a tabloid. We might modify our thoughts based on what they are carrying with them, a bag, a ruck-sac, a briefcase. Do they carry or wear their coat or hat or jacket? Are they on their own or with a companion?

How often has a person then spoken to you and you realise that you had either totally misjudged them or actually guessed correctly. We set a lot of store by first impressions, love at first sight, our first instincts, but it is skill you need to hone and even then you might not always get it right!

The Dalai Lama is reputed to have said that "Sometimes one creates a dynamic impression by saying something, and sometimes one creates as significant an impression by remaining silent." Truly wise words!

November 10, 2007 - Two visionary men

Yesterday I visited the Lincoln Memorial for the first time. Having ascended to the memorial I was taken by the simplistic beauty of the building.

The statue of Lincoln was so classically carved, representing him as serene and with such strong lines. His right hand looked a little too large, but maybe that was to define his strength of character as it gripped the chair. His right foot stretched out from the step as though he was slightly impatient and wanted to rise from the chair and continue with his work.

The building was filled with sound, a cacophony of laughter, shouts and noise with people taking photographs of each other, their families, school visits; it definitely wasn't a reverent atmosphere. I wasn't too sure about this ambience to begin with, but then I thought that maybe Lincoln's hopes were that he would leave a legacy where people would just live their lives; that he would place the foundations for a nation that would not be concerned about what had gone before, who were free to express their joy of living.

Maybe he hoped that his legacy would be an optimistic light so that future generations would not have to focus on the dark times that he had overseen during the civil war when a nation was divided.

As I turned to leave and walked towards and down the steps I was very aware that I was following in the footsteps too of Martin Luther King. In my mind I could almost conjure up the crowds that had been there that day in August 1963 standing between the two lines of trees listening to him speak. His "I have a dream" speech is iconic and in the exhibition inside the Lincoln Memorial his words were ringing out.

I am so glad that I went to the memorial on a rainy, overcast day to pay my respects to two men of great belief and great insight, who also had such hope that their fellow man would ultimately do what, was right and just.

November 10, 2007 - Remembering the fallen

I visited the Vietnam Memorial in Washington almost on Veterans Day, or as we call it in the UK Armistice Day. The path to the memorial was very crowded with many former veterans, who were grouped together some talking, some lost in their mutual thoughts.

When I got to the memorial people were reading out the names that were on the stones, remembering the fallen. I was struck by how simple and yet how emotive the memorial was. It was designed so that the first few stones that you walked by were relatively small and just contained a few names. As you walked further the stones seemed to rise from the base each one with more names than the one before and the height of the stones increased until they were well above your head.

When the stones were standing taller than me and filled with hundreds of names the enormity of the loss of life was brought home, strongly and quite starkly.

What made the experience even more poignant was I fell into step quite unintentionally with a veteran. He was immaculately turned out I guess in his early sixties and he held a small piece of paper in his hand. When he found a name on the tablets he was looking for he slowly ran his fingertips across the lettering, feeling the etched indentations in a slowly measured way. I could tell that he was lost in his thoughts remembering the living, breathing person who those words represented. For me the memorial was moving and poignant, but to him and many others they were real people who they had lost and despite the passage of time their loss was still heavy in their hearts. He repeated this tribute three or four times.

As I walked on, the stones slowly decreased in size again until each contained just a few names. I then saw him walk off quietly into the cool autumn afternoon. What I experienced will stay with me forever.

November 11, 2007 - Collaborative decision making

It was interesting for me when reading some of Abraham Lincoln's speeches how much he believed in the strength of the Union. He wanted to overcome the policies and issues that divided the Union in order to celebrate and increase the principles that held it together.

Should we take a lesson from history? Should we concentrate on what we have in common with others rather than what divides us and causes individuals and groups to become entrenched?

Is collaborative thinking and decision making a process we should undertake more often in our work and private lives? Collaborative thinking and decision making is the interaction between individuals with the aim of meeting a common goal, but often coming initially from different positions or opinions. Collaborative thinking requires effective and honest communication, free sharing of information and then cooperation in developing, negotiating and coordinated a mutually satisfying conclusion.

Sounds like pie-in-the-sky? Many would think so, but the truth is unless we use this approach in our work lives we will continue to battle against unresolved issues that can often divide and undermine a project, team or organisation.

November 13, 2007 - Musing on musings

For my Nuffield Scholarship, I have carried around a little moleskin notebook, well several over the five weeks. As I have spent quite a lot of time on my own with my thoughts, I have found myself writing in a way I haven't done since I was a teenager.

People do give you strange looks when you are scribbling in your notebook in a cafe or on a train. However, JK Rowling reputedly wrote the first Harry Potter book in a cafe, so I am in good company. When I get home I will be able to express myself verbally again so I wonder if my writing will diminish. The strange thing is when I was a teenager I didn't want anyone to read my musings. Now I find myself publishing them on a blog! Why tell the world? Why believe that others will actually want to read our thoughts? Is it just the height of egotism? Maybe it is egotistical, but I am not alone because there are millions of people doing the same in their blogs every day. I think that as humans we feel a basic need to communicate and we also seek recognition by others of our thoughts and opinions. Historically, that was from people close to us, but now we have the technology to broadcast our ideas to all corners of the earth.

www.ingramcontent.com/pod-product-compliance
Lightning Source LLC
Chambersburg PA
CBHW021022090426
42738CB00007B/871